Big Mud Run

Written by Zoë Clarke

Collins

We can go on a mud run.

mud

Get set and go!

We dash off!

5

Then we jog and zig-zag.

6

hop

We hang on and kick.

thin rungs

We sink in the mud.

mud bank

We rush to win.

We are quick!

/qu/

14

/w/

 Review: After reading

Use your assessment from hearing the children read to choose any GPCs, words or tricky words that need additional practice.

Read 1: Decoding
- Look at pages 12 and 13 together. Ask the children:
  - Can you find a word that begins with the /w/ phoneme? (*win*) Now sound out the word and blend the sounds together. (*w/i/n – **win***)
  - Can you find a word that begins with the /qu/ phoneme? (*quick*) Now sound out the word and blend the sounds together. (*qu/i/ck – **quick***)
- Look at the "I spy sounds" pages (14–15) together. How many words can the children point out that contain the /w/ sound or the /qu/ sound? (*winner, wet, quench, quick*)

Read 2: Prosody
- Model reading each page with expression to the children.
- After you have read each page, ask the children to have a go at reading with expression.

Read 3: Comprehension
- For every question ask the children how they know the answer. Ask:
  - What would you have to do on each of the obstacles in the mud run? (*walk over the rope bridge, walk along the seesaw, climb over the mud bank, crawl under the tunnel*)
  - Which of the obstacles or the activities in the pictures do you think would be most difficult, and why?
  - Would you like to do a mud run? Why, or why not?